COLOUR

COLOR

COULEUR

FARBE

AUTHORS
Fernando de Haro & Omar Fuentes

EDITORIAL DESIGN & PRODUCTION
AM Editores S.A. de C.V.

PROJECT MANAGERS
Edali Nuñez Daniel
Laura Mijares Castellá

COORDINATION
Dulce Ma. Rodríguez Flores

PREPRESS COORDINATION
Carolina Medina Granados

COPYWRITER
Roxana Villalobos

ENGLISH TRANSLATION
Babel International Translators

FRENCH TRANSLATION
Architextos: Translation Service and Language Solutions

GERMAN TRANSLATION
Angloamericano de Cuernavaca
Sabine Klein

100+ TIPS · IDEAS
colour . color
couleur . farbe

© 2011, Fernando de Haro & Omar Fuentes
AM Editores S.A. de C.V.
Paseo de Tamarindos 400 B, suite 109, Col. Bosques de las Lomas,
C.P. 05120, México, D.F., Tel. 52(55) 5258 0279
ame@ameditores.com / **www.ameditores.com**

ISBN 13: 978-607-437-084-3

Printed in China.

INTRODUCTION

INTRODUCCIÓN

INTRODUCTION

EINLEITUNG

When it comes to architecture, interior design and decoration, color is an absolute must and using it properly becomes a satisfying challenge.

Color is the tool professionals turn to for effects such as accentuating the elevation of buildings, pronouncing depth, creating an impression of temperature, defining focal points, generating a rhythm, proposing moods, seeking out contrasts and complements, turning the brilliance of a given atmosphere up or down, emphasizing or concealing parts or objects, among a whole host of other objectives. Color tones need to be used to full effect if the decor is to be a success, which is why all the possible combinations need to be studied in order to find the best option for the ambience sought. It is crucial to consider the home's orientation, as well as the inflow of sunlight and the design of artificial lighting. At the end of the day, color would not exist without light and only comes into being through its interaction with light. The shape and size of the room are equally important factors, as are the look of the furniture, the way the space in question will be used and the desired sensory, ambient and optical characteristics.

This book provides tips, pointers and solutions from top designers for users who want to employ color to its full potential around the house.

Para la arquitectura, el diseño interior y la decoración, el uso del color es una necesidad y su manipulación se convierte en un atractivo reto.

Los profesionales recurren al color para conseguir efectos tales como acentuar la volumetría de las edificaciones, señalar profundidades, proponer alguna impresión de temperatura, generar puntos focales, crear un ritmo, sugerir estados de ánimo, buscar contrastes y armonías, aumentar o disminuir la luminosidad de una atmósfera, destacar o disimular las partes u objetos, entre una vasta lista.

De la buena aplicación de los matices cromáticos depende el éxito decorativo que se alcance; por ello es necesario estudiar las posibles combinaciones y ver cuál es la que mejor se ajusta al ambiente que se busca. Es de suma importancia considerar la orientación de la casa, así como las entradas de luz natural y el diseño de la iluminación artificial. A fin de cuentas, el color no existiría sin la luz ya que es un fenómeno que se deriva de la interacción con ésta. También es relevante la dimensión y la forma de la habitación, el aspecto de los muebles, el uso al que se destina el espacio y las características sensoriales, anímicas y ópticas que se le desean dar.

Este libro presenta algunos tips, consejos y soluciones a los que han llegado los diseñadores para usar adecuadamente el color en las diversas áreas de la casa.

Pour l'architecture, le design intérieur et la décoration, la couleur est une nécessité et savoir l'utiliser un défi agréable à relever parce qu'elle sert à de multiples choses.

Les professionnels font ainsi appel à la couleur pour concevoir certains effets comme, entre autres, accentuer la volumétrie de la construction, mettre en valeur les profondeurs, déterminer des températures variées, créer des contrastes, des harmonies, un rythme, des points dans l'espace qui attirent l'œil, suggérer différentes atmosphères, augmenter ou diminuer la luminosité d'une pièce, faire ressortir ou dissimuler certaines parties. La réussite d'une décoration dépend en grande partie des gammes chromatiques employées. Il est donc indispensable de bien étudier les combinaisons possibles et de choisir celles qui correspondront le mieux à l'atmosphère envisagée. Aussi est-il essentiel de déterminer au préalable l'orientation de la maison, les sources de lumière naturelle et le design de l'éclairage artificiel. En fin de compte, la couleur n'existe pas sans la lumière car elle résulte de son interaction avec cette dernière. Les dimensions et la forme des pièces jouent également un rôle, tout comme la fonction qu'on leur attribue, les caractéristiques de l'atmosphère que l'on souhaite installer, les particularités sensorielles et visuelles de l'espace et l'apparence des meubles.

Dans ce livre, on trouvera donc quelques astuces, conseils, solutions que les designers ont élaborés pour que chacun puisse correctement utiliser la couleur dans les diverses pièces de sa demeure.

In der Architektur, dem Innendesign und der Dekoration, werden notwendigerweise Farben verwendet und ihre Handhabung stellt eine attraktive Herausforderung dar.

Fachleute greifen auf Farben zurück, um Effekte, wie die Grösse eines Gebäudes, herauszustellen, räumliche Tiefe zu betonen, das Temperaturempfinden zu beeinflussen, Blickpunkte zu schaffen, Rhythmus entstehen zu lassen, eine Stimmung anzuregen, Kontrast und Harmonie zu suchen, die Helligkeit zu erhöhen oder zu verringern, Objekte oder Zonen zu betonen oder zu kaschieren und vieles andere mehr.

Von einer guten Anwendung der Farbtöne hängt der Erfolg der Dekoration ab; deshalb ist es notwendig die möglichen Kombinationen zu kennen und zu wissen, welche sich am besten für das gewünschte Ambiente eignen. Es ist sehr wichtig, die Ausrichtung des Hauses zu beachten, so wie auch den natürlichen Lichteinfall und das Design der künstlichen Beleuchtung. Letztendlich gibt es ohne Licht keine Farbe, da sie ein Produkt der Zusammenwirkung mit Licht ist. Auch wichtig sind die Ausmasse und die Form des Raumes, das Aussehen der Möbel, die Nutzung des Raumes und die sinnlichen Eigenschaften, gefühlsmässige und optische, die man dem Raum geben möchte.

Dieses Buch stellt einige Tipps, Ratschläge und Lösungen vor, zu denen Innendekorateure gelangt sind, um Farben in den verschiedenen Bereichen des Hauses angemessen einzusetzen.

LIVING AND DINING ROOMS
SALAS Y COMEDORES
CHAMBRES ET SALLES À MANGER
WOHN- UND ESSZIMMER

The color of a space is one of the basic elements that conform a design. There are many ways to obtain a comfortable and pleasant atmosphere in a living room or dining room; it all really boils down to personal preference. It can be achieved using a single color, a scale of colors or color combinations. Regardless of the choice made, the furniture must be taken into account. Some styles don't combine well with certain tones. For instance, if a black or slate gray tone is chosen for the walls, the decor will be more slanted towards a contemporary ambience in which furniture made with pure lines and right angles is the best bet. Rustic style seats or armchairs, on the other hand, combine well with earth tones. Neutral tones on large surfaces – walls, floors and ceilings – open up many possibilities for using color on furniture and fittings, and it is also easier to clearly define an atmosphere. The color of light and artwork will also weave its spell on the overall setting.

El color de un espacio es uno de los elementos esenciales en la composición del diseño. Hay muchas maneras de llegar a un ambiente confortable y agradable en una sala o un comedor; en realidad, todo depende de las preferencias personales de cada uno; se puede hacer con un solo color, basándose en una gama o bien con combinaciones.

Cual sea la alternativa que se escoja, es conveniente tener en cuenta el mobiliario. Hay estilos que van bien con determinados tonos, por ejemplo, si se elige un matiz negro o pizarra para muros, se está inclinando el decorado hacia una atmósfera contemporánea, en donde los muebles de línea puras y ángulos rectos son idóneos. Por el contrario, para unas sillas o sillones rústicos son muy adecuadas las gamas térreas.

Desde luego, si se procuran las tonalidades neutras para las grandes superficies —muros, pisos y techos— las posibilidades de jugar con los colores en el mobiliario y los accesorios aumentan, pero también se consigue con mayor facilidad la mesura de una atmósfera. Asimismo el color de la luz y el del arte, tienen efectos en el conjunto.

La couleur d'un espace est un des éléments essentiels propre à la composition du design. On peut parvenir à créer une ambiance confortable et agréable dans un salon ou une salle à manger de plusieurs façons. Mais, en réalité, tout est d'abord basé sur les goûts personnels de chacun. Et on peut opter pour une couleur unique, une gamme précise ou, bien évidemment, pour des associations.

Quelle que soit l'option retenue, il ne faut pas oublier de prendre en compte le mobilier. En effet, certains styles de meubles ne conviennent pas à des teintes déterminées. Par exemple, avec du noir ou du gris ardoise sur les murs, on cherchera plutôt à donner à la pièce une atmosphère moderne par l'intermédiaire de meubles à lignes pures et à angles droits. En revanche, si l'on dispose de chaises ou fauteuils de style rustique, une gamme de couleurs terre sera tout indiquée.

Il est évident que si l'on peut appliquer des teintes neutres sur les grandes surfaces (murs, sol, plafond), les possibilités de jouer avec les couleurs du mobilier et des accessoires seront plus importantes mais on pourra également parvenir à une atmosphère précise plus facilement. Enfin, n'oublions pas que la lumière et les objets d'art jouent aussi un rôle dans l'ensemble.

Die Farbe eines Bereiches ist eine der wesentlichen Elemente in der Komposition des Designs. Es gibt viele Möglichkeiten zu einem freundlichen und angenehmen Ambiente in einem Wohn- oder einem Esszimmer zu gelangen; in Wirklichkeit hängt alles von den persönlichen Vorzügen jedes einzelnen ab; man kann alles in einer Farbe halten, sich auf ein Farbspektrum beschränken oder auch kombinieren.

Welche Möglichkeit man auch wählt, man sollte die Möblierung bedenken. Es gibt Stile, die nicht gut zu bestimmten Farbtönen passen; zum Beispiel, wenn man einen schwarzen oder schieferfarbenen Ton für die Wände wählt, bietet sich eine zeitgenössische Atmosphäre an, in der die Möbel von reinen Linien und rechte Winkel ideal sind. Im Gegensatz dazu, sind für rustikale Stühle oder Sessel Farbspektren in Erdtönen angemessen.

Wenn man jedoch auf den grossen Oberflächen – Wände, Böden und Decke – neutrale Farbtöne wählt, vergrössern sich die Möglichkeiten mit den Farben der Möbel und Dekorationsgegenständen zu spielen und man kann leichter eine bestimmte Atmosphäre herstellen. Die Farbe des Lichts und der Kunstwerke hat auch einen Effekt auf die Gesamtkomposition.

TIPS - ASTUCES - TIPPS

- *White surfaces increase the sensation of brilliance when they come into contact with light.*
- *Las superficies blancas aumentan la sensación de luminosidad al contacto con la luz.*
- *Au contact de la lumière, les surfaces blanches renforcent la sensation de luminosité dans la pièce.*
- *Weisse Oberflächen erhöhen beim Kontakt mit Licht den Eindruck von Helligkeit.*

A work of art or
a set of books
can provide a
note of color
in a neutral
atmosphere.

Une œuvre d'art ou
un groupe de livres
peuvent constituer
une touche de couleur
dans une atmosphère
neutre.

Una obra de arte
o un grupo de
libros pueden ser
la nota de color
en una atmósfera
neutra.

Ein Kunstwerk oder
eine Ansammlung
Bücher können
einer neutralen
Atmosphäre eine
farbige Note
geben.

Different white
and beige tones
give rise to an
uncomplicated
ambience in
which serenity
reigns supreme.

Distintos tonos
blanquecinos
y beiges
conforman un
ambiente sobrio
provocando una
sensación de
serenidad.

Les dégradés
de blanc et de
beige donnent
naissance à
une pièce sobre
qui respire la
sérénité.

Unterschiedliche
weissliche und
beigefarbene
Töne schaffen
ein nüchternes
Ambiente, ein
Gefühl von Ruhe
hervorrufend.

TIPS - ASTUCES - TIPPS
• Black details in a setting dominated by light tones will become focal points.
• Un accesorio negro en un contexto de tonos claros se convierte en el punto focal.
• Un accessoire noir dans un ensemble dominé par des teintes claires retient l'œil.
• Ein schwarzes Objekt, in einer Umgebung heller Farbtöne, wird zum Blickfang.

A rug with stripes or bands of color will liven up an otherwise tranquil living room.

Un tapete de franjas de colores la da vida a una estancia que posee un diseño sereno.

Un tapis en couleur et à franges apporte un peu de vie dans un séjour au design sobre.

Ein Teppich mit farbigen Streifen lässt ein Wohnzimmer mit ruhigem Design lebendig wirken.

TIPS - ASTUCES - TIPPS

• Chocolate and raw tones combine exquisitely, while stainless steel emphasizes the room's contemporary feel.
• La mezcla de chocolate y matices crudos es sobria; el acero inoxidable acentúa el aire contemporáneo.
• Associer la couleur chocolat à des tons écrus reste sobre et l'acier inoxydable souligne l'aspect moderne de la pièce.
• Die Mischung aus Schokoladenbraun und Naturtönen ist nüchtern; der rostfreie Stahl betont die zeitgenössische Atmosphäre.

TIPS - ASTUCES - TIPPS
- *Pure white door and window trims and blinds will produce a wonderful luminous effect.*
- *Si las molduras de puertas y ventanas al igual que las persianas son blanco puro el efecto luminoso es increíble.*
- *Si les moulures des portes et fenêtres sont en blanc pur, tout comme les stores, la luminosité créée est incroyable.*
- *Wenn die Rahmen der Türen und Fenster, wie auch die Jalousien, von reinem Weiss sind, ist der Effekt auf die Helligkeit unglaublich.*

The color of
wood affords
warmth for a
dining room in
pale tones.

La couleur du
bois réchauffe
une salle à
manger dominée
par des teintes
claires.

El color de
la madera le
aporta calidez
a un comedor
dominado por
tonos claros.

Die Farbe des
Holzes steuert in
einem Esszimmer,
in dem helle Töne
vorherrschen,
Wärme bei.

A brightly colored object or work of art at the back of a space will emphasize its depth.

En plaçant une oeuvre d'art de couleurs vives dans une pièce pour capter les regards, on met en valeur sa profondeur.

Al colocar un objeto o pieza de arte de color recio en el remate de un espacio se subraya la profundidad de éste.

Durch das Anbringen eines Kunstobjektes in einer kräftigen Farbe am Ende eines Raumes, betont man dessen Tiefe.

A few orange cushions heighten the perception of vitality in the dining room.

Unos cojines en naranja sólido le otorgan al comedor una mayor impresión de energía.

Quelques coussins orange vif dynamisent un peu plus la salle à manger.

Einige Kissen in reinem Orange geben dem Esszimmer eine energiereichere Atmosphäre.

TIPS - ASTUCES - TIPPS
• A visual flow can be created in the area with a few points of contrasting color.
• Con puntos de algún color contrastante se genera un recorrido visual en el área.
• Quelques touches de couleur contrastante incitent à parcourir toute la pièce du regard.
• Mit verschiedenen Zonen in kontrastierenden Farben lädt man zu einer optischen Reise durch den Bereich ein.

The decor
exudes a natural
and harmonious
quality when its
colors echo those
of nature.

Una decoración
con gesto de
naturalidad
y armonía se
consigue imitando
el colorido de
la naturaleza.

On parvient à
une décoration
qui rappelle
l'harmonie de la
nature en utilisant
les couleurs des
végétaux.

Eine Dekoration
mit natürlichem
Ausdruck und
Harmonie,
erreicht man
durch die
Nachahmung der
Farben der Natur.

TIPS - ASTUCES - TIPPS
- The tones of wood and natural fibers perform a substantial role in the decor.
- El matiz de la madera y las fibras naturales tiene peso en el decorado.
- Les tons et les veines naturelles du bois jouent un rôle important dans le décor.
- Die Schattierungen des Holzes und der Naturfasern haben in der Dekoration Gewicht.

The combination of black, red and beige will always afford stylish results.

Negro, rojo y beige es una combinación con la que siempre se llega a un resultado elegante.

Sil'on associe le noir, le rouge et le beige, on parvient toujours à un résultat élégant.

Schwarz, Rot und Beige ist eine Kombination, mit der man immer ein elegantes Ergebnis erzielt.

TIPS - ASTUCES - TIPPS
- *A work of art in lively colors helps create a gregarious ambience in the dining room.*
- *Una pieza de arte de colores vibrantes coopera a crear un ánimo de convivencia en el comedor.*
- *Une peinture de couleurs vives participe à l'atmosphère conviviale qui règne dans la salle à manger.*
- *Fin Kunstwerk in leuchtenden Farben hilft im Esszimmer eine gesellige Stimmung zu schaffen.*

Bright red and orange pool efforts with wood to infuse a living room with warmth.

Un mueble donde las tonalidades encendidas del rojo y el naranja en conjunto con la madera provocan movimiento visual.

Les reflets enflammés du rouge et de l'orange, associés au bois, donnent l'impression que la pièce se réchauffe.

Das leuchtende Rot und Orange, zusammen mit dem Holz, lassen das Wohnzimmer warm wirken.

TIPS - ASTUCES - TIPPS
• Seats are very attractive when upholstered in a color with presence.
• Unas sillas tapizadas en un color con personalidad se vuelven muy atractivas.
• Quelques chaises personnalisées de couleur vive sont très esthétiques dans un séjour.
• Einige Stühle, mit Bezügen in einer Farbe mit Persönlichkeit, wirken sehr attraktiv.

Red should be used carefully because it has a habit of making spaces look smaller than they actually are.

La aplicación del rojo debe ser medida, ya que tiende a disminuir visualmente el espacio, haciendo que parezca más pequeño.

L'utilisation du rouge doit rester modeste car cette couleur a tendance à réduire l'espace et les pièces ont l'air plus petit.

Rot sollte man nur vorsichtig verwenden, da es dazu neigt, die optische Grösse zu verringern, wodurch ein Raum kleiner wirkt.

TIPS - ASTUCES - TIPPS
- *A good balance between red, gray, white and black will create a splendid ambience.*
- *Cuando el rojo, el gris, el blanco y el negro están en equilibrio entre sí, dan ambientes deliciosos.*
- *Lorsqu'il y a équilibre entre le rouge, le gris, le blanc et le noir, leur association est très esthétique dans une pièce.*
- *Wenn Rot, Grau, Weiss und Schwarz im Gleichgewicht stehen, entsteht ein charmantes Ambiente.*

Lavender has a soothing effect. When combined with pale tones it looks lively, while darker tones make it more stylish.

El lavanda es un matiz relajante que con tonos claros luce alegre y con oscuros se vuelve más elegante.

Le mauve est relaxant. Associé à des teintes claires, il est distrayant; avec des couleurs foncées, il est plus esthétique.

Lavendel ist ein entspannender Farbton, der kombiniert mit hellen Tönen fröhlich und mit dunklen elegant wirkt.

TIPS - ASTUCES - TIPPS

- *Violet upholstery can disguise the narrowness of a living room.*
- *Las tapicerías violetas son una opción para disimular la estrechez de una sala.*
- *Les tissus violets représentent un bon moyen de faire oublier l'étroitesse d'un salon.*
- *Violette Bezüge sind eine Möglichkeit, die Enge eines Wohnzimmers zu überspielen.*

TIPS - ASTUCES - TIPPS
- A good blend of warm and cold colors fine tunes the chromatic temperature of a room.
- Para afinar la temperatura de un sitio hay que mezclar colores fríos y cálidos.
- En mélangeant les couleurs froides et chaudes dans une pièce, on équilibre la température de l'atmosphère qui y règne.
- Um das Temperaturempfinden in einem Bereich zu verfeinern, mischt man kalte mit warmen Farben.

Lilac textiles provide a dramatic touch and plenty of personality to wooden dining room furniture.

Los textiles lilas le dan un toque de dramatismo y personalidad a un comedor de madera.

Les tissus couleur lilas renforcent et personnalisent l'atmosphère d'une salle à manger dominée par le bois.

Lila Stoffe geben einem Esszimmer aus Holz eine dramatische Note und Persönlichkeit.

Some colors just
merge into the
landscape
to harmonize
the indoor and
outdoor areas.

Algunos colores
pueden fundirse
con el paisaje,
logrando armonía
entre interior
y exterior.

Quelques couleurs
peuvent se fondre
dans le paysage
environnant et
harmoniser l'intérieur
avec l'extérieur.

Einige Farben scheinen
mit der Landschaft
zu verschmelzen,
damit Harmonie
zwischen dem Innen
und Aussenbereich
schaffend.

TIPS - ASTUCES - TIPPS
- *A couple of seats with a floral pattern and lively tones will become a focal point in the room.*
- *Un par de sillones con estampado floral se convierten en los puntos focales si el tono es atrevido.*
- *Deux fauteuils avec des motifs à fleurs peuvent devenir l'élément - clé de la pièce si leurs couleurs sont originales.*
- *Ein Paar Sessel mit Blumenmuster werden zum Blickfang, wenn ihre Farbe gewagt ist.*

An atmosphere reminiscent of nature is obtained if the living room is decorated with a pallet of brown and green tones.

Decorar una sala dentro de la gama cafés y canelas con tonos de verde conduce a una atmósfera que recuerda a la naturaleza.

Utiliser, pour un salon, une gamme chromatique marron et cannelle avec quelques touches de vert dote la pièce d'une atmosphère qui rappelle celle de la nature.

Ein Wohnzimmer in Braun - und Zimttönen, mit einigen Grüntönen zu dekorieren, führt zu einer Atmosphäre, die an die Natur erinnert.

TIPS - ASTUCES - TIPPS
• Green tones used on upholstery are highlighted with the white on the walls and the wood's brown tones.
• Los tonos de verde de una tapicería se realzan con el blanco de los muros y el café de la madera.
• Les reflets verts des chaises ressortent avec le blanc des murs et le marron du bois.
• Die Grüntöne der Bezüge fallen durch das Weiss der Wände und dem Braun des Holzes besonders auf.

TIPS - ASTUCES - TIPPS
- *Cold tones emphasize spaciousness.*
- *Las tonalidades frías evocan una mayor amplitud del espacio.*
- *Les teintes froides agrandissent une pièce.*
- *Kühle Farbtöne erwecken den Eindruck grösserer räumlicher Weite.*

Aquatic tones are cold. When they are used, the sensation of warmth needs to be increased by including creams and/or wood tones.

Los tonos aqua son fríos, si se introducen hay que incrementar la sensación de calidez incluyendo matices cremas y/o madera.

Le vert d'eau est très froid. Si on l'emploie, il faut essayer de réchauffer les lieux avec des teintes crème et/ou du bois.

Wassertöne sind kalt, wenn man sie benutzt, sollte man den Eindruck von Wärme durch Cremetöne und/oder Holz erhöhen.

KITCHENS
COCINAS
CUISINES
KÜCHEN

The use of color in the kitchen is defined by a number of different aspects, one of the main ones being a sense of cleanliness and other sensations specifically required by a kitchen. Then there are also the tones of the different surfaces in the preparation area and the glints and glimmers they generate.

The color pallet chosen for this space should offer some degree of comfort. It is essential not to undermine luminosity in the kitchen because light is indispensable for cooking. The area should also look as appealing as possible, considering its measurements, shape and functions.

Current trends dictate using fewer tones in the décor or even just a single color scale, which is usually combined with the natural tones of building materials.

It is also a good idea to carefully choose where color will be applied. Sometimes, cabinets are the best option, and on other occasions it is on the walls or floor. Colorful ceilings are not a common choice.

Es evidente que el uso del color en la cocina obedece a una multiplicidad de aspectos; entre los que más cuentan están la percepción de limpieza y otras sensaciones que se busquen del sitio, la tonalidad de cada una de las cubiertas de las áreas de preparado y el reflejo que provoquen los acabados de éstas.

La paleta cromática que se elija para este espacio debe ofrecer un grado de confort; es básico no restar luminosidad a esta habitación, pues la luz es indispensable para cocinar; así como dotar a esta zona de la mejor estética posible, considerando sus dimensiones, su forma y su funcionalidad.

Actualmente existe la tendencia a no introducir demasiadas tonalidades en la composición decorativa de la cocina o incluso a limitarla a una gama, que generalmente se mezcla con los de los matices naturales de los materiales de construcción.

Asimismo, es necesario analizar bien en dónde ajusta colocar la nota de color, algunas veces lo mejor es que sea en los gabinetes de los muebles, otras en los muros o en el piso, siendo en general muy poco frecuentes los techos coloridos.

La couleur d'une cuisine doit bien évidemment correspondre à ce que l'on espère dans une telle pièce. Il faut, d'abord, que la sensation de propre y règne mais ce n'est pas la seule car la teinte de chaque revêtement employé dans la zone de travail et les reflets produits par certaines finitions jouent un rôle.

La palette chromatique choisie pour cet espace doit aussi être pratique. Il faut donc qu'il y ait de la luminosité, indispensable pour cuisiner, mais également une certaine esthétique dans la mesure du possible et en vertu des dimensions, de la forme et de la fonctionnalité de l'endroit.

Actuellement, les tendances vont vers un emploi limité de couleurs pour la décoration d'une cuisine. On préconise même parfois de se limiter à une seule gamme chromatique qui s'associera aux teintes naturelles des matériaux de construction.

Mais, comme partout ailleurs, il est indispensable de bien choisir l'emplacement de la touche de couleur. On la placera quelquefois sur les portes des placards, sur les murs, au sol mais très rarement au plafond.

Es ist offensichtlich, dass die Verwendung von Farbe in der Küche einer Vielzahl von Aspekten unterliegt; die Wichtigsten sind der Eindruck von Sauberkeit und andere Empfindungen, die man in diesem Bereich sucht, der Farbton jeder einzelnen Oberfläche bei den Arbeitsflächen und deren Reflektionen.

Die Farbpalette, die für diesen Bereich gewählt wird, sollte einen gewissen Komfort bieten; es ist essentiell diesem Bereich nicht die Helligkeit zu entziehen, da sie unerlässlich zum Kochen ist; so wie auch dem Bereich die höchstmögliche Ästhetik zu verleihen, seine Grösse, seine Form und seine Funktionalität berücksichtigend.

Gegenwärtig gibt es die Tendenz nicht zu viele Farbtöne in der Dekoration der Küche zu verwenden oder sich sogar auf nur ein Farbspektrum zu beschränken, das sich normalerweise mit den natürlichen Schattierungen der Baumaterialen mischt.

Ausserdem sollte man gut analysieren wo eine Farbnote gesetzt werden sollte, manchmal ist es besser, das auf den Türen der Möbel zu machen, manchmal auf den Wänden oder auf dem Boden, farbige Decken dagegen sind nicht sehr üblich.

White is the best bet for a long, narrow area because it creates a sensation of spaciousness.

El blanco es el color más provechoso para un espacio estrecho y largo, pues aumenta la impresión de amplitud.

Le blanc est la couleur la plus utilisée pour un espace long et étroit car il donne l'impression d'agrandir la pièce.

Weiss ist die vorteilhafteste Farbe für einen engen und langen Raum, da es den Eindruck von Weite erhöht.

TIPS - ASTUCES - TIPPS
- *White kitchens look tidy and peaceful, both of which are important qualities in this area.*
- *Los cocinas blancas dan la apariencia de pulcritud y serenidad, propiedades esenciales en esta área.*
- *Les cuisines de couleur blanche ont l'air plus net, plus calme et correspondent ainsi à ce que l'on espère trouver dans cette pièce.*
- *Weisse Küchen wirken sauber und freundlich, wesentliche Eigenschaften dieses Bereiches.*

TIPS - ASTUCES - TIPPS
- Any dark surfaces should ideally be on the same wall that light comes in through or parallel to it.
- Conviene que las superficies oscuras se encuentren en el mismo muro de las entradas de luz.
- Lorsque certaines surfaces sont foncées, il vaut mieux qu'elles se situent près des sources de lumière naturelle ou parallèlement à celles-ci
- Wenn es dunkle Oberflächen gibt, sollten sie sich auf der gleichen Wand wie die Fenster oder parallel zu ihnen befinden.

White furniture designed with pure and simple lines suggests a contemporary setting.

El mobiliario de líneas puras y simples en color blanco evoca un ambiente contemporáneo.

Un mobilier blanc à lignes pures et simples donne à la cuisine un air très moderne.

Möbel mit klaren und einfachen Linien in Weiss schaffen ein zeitgenössisches Ambiente.

TIPS · ASTUCES · TIPPS
- Bright red is an extreme tone that should be used in moderation in the kitchen.
- El rojo encendido es un tono extremo que conviene aplicar moderadamente en la cocina.
- Le rouge vif est une couleur délicate à utiliser et il est préférable d'y avoir recours avec parcimonie dans la cuisine.
- Leuchtendes Rot ist ein extremer Farbton, der nur mit Mässigkeit in der Küche verwendet werden sollte.

A shared
space will be
brought to life
with a few
items of red
furniture.

Incluir algunos
muebles en rojo
le imprimen
movimiento
y alegría a
un espacio
compartido.

Placer quelques
meubles rouges
apporte un peu
de mouvement et
de gaité dans une
pièce commune
dominé par le bois.

Ein multifunktioneller
Bereich bekommt
durch einige rote
Möbelstücke
Bewegung und
wirkt lebhafter.

A wall in granite tones highlights the depth of its plane and has a very persuasive effect on the eye.

Un muro en una tonalidad granate subraya la profundidad del plano en el que se encuentra y se vuelve persuasivo para la vista.

Un mur de teinte grenat met en valeur la profondeur de la surface où il se trouve et attire l'œil.

Eine Wand in Granatrot unterstreicht die Tiefe des Grundrisses und ist verführerisch fürs Auge.

TIPS - ASTUCES - TIPPS
• *Cold colors such as blue, green, lilac and violet help regulate the temperature in a warm setting.*
• *La introducción de colores fríos como el lila o violeta coopera a nivelar la temperatura de un ambiente cálido.*
• *L'emploi de couleurs froides – bleu, vert, lilas, violet· équilibre l'atmosphère dans une pièce dominée par des teintes chaudes.*
• *Das Einführen kalter Farben – Blau, Grün, Lila und Violett – hilft die Temperatur eines warmen Ambientes auszugleichen.*

Bright orange and pure white provide a balanced combination for furniture.

Una alternativa equilibrada se deriva de combinar el anaranjado destellante y el blanco puro en los muebles.

Une solution existe pour équilibrer une cuisine : associer, pour les meubles, un orange brillant avec du blanc pur.

Eine ausgewogene Alternative besteht in der Kombination von leuchtendem Orange und reinem Weiss bei den Möbeln.

TIPS · ASTUCES · TIPPS

• Orange is ideal for infusing a generous measure of vitality and personality into the kitchen.
• El anaranjado es perfecto para dotar de vitalidad y personalidad a una cocina.
• Couleur infaillible, l'orange est parfait pour dynamiser et personnaliser une cuisine.
• Orange ist perfekt, um der Küche Leben zu verleihen und unfehlbar, um ihr Persönlichkeit zu geben.

TIPS - ASTUCES - TIPPS
- Pink lends modern kitchens a retro or vintage air.
- El rosa le da un aire retro a una cocina moderna.
- Le rose donne un air rétro et authentique à une cuisine moderne.
- Rosa gibt einer modernen Küche einen Hauch Retro oder Vintage Stil.

An audacious
blend of gray,
pink, white and
wood gives the
kitchen presence.

Una combinación
atrevida de gris,
rosa, blanco
y madera le
confiere fuerza a
la cocina.

L'association
assez osée entre
le gris, le rose,
le blanc et le
marron du bois
dote la cuisine
d'une certaine
force.

Eine gewagte
Kombination
von Grau, Rosa,
Weiss und Holz
gibt der Küche
optische Stärke.

Black chairs and a white tablecloth are the ultimate expression of contrast in the dining room and invariably a refined choice.

Sillas negras y cubierta de mesa blanca es la máxima imagen del contraste en un comedor que siempre resulta refinado.

Des sièges noirs et une table laquée en blanc offrent un contraste du plus bel effet dans une salle à manger et font ressortir son élégance.

Schwarze Stühle und eine weisse Tischplatte sind der grösstmögliche Kontrast in einem Esszimmer und wirken immer raffinert.

TIPS - ASTUCES - TIPPS
- The vibrant tones of flowers are always welcome in the décor.
- Los tonos vibrantes de las flores son siempre un aliado en la decoración.
- On peut toujours compter sur les teintes vives des fleurs, véritables alliées dans la décoration.
- Die kräftigen Farben von Blumen sind immer ein Verbündeter in der Dekoration.

If the kitchen design is completely black, then as many sources of direct and indirect daylight and artificial light as possible need to be defined.

Si se diseña una cocina totalmente negra, hay que buscar la mayor cantidad de fuentes de luz natural o artificial, directa e indirecta.

Si l'on envisage une cuisine entièrement noire, il est indispensable de prévoir le plus grand nombre possible de sources de lumière, naturelle ou artificielle, directe ou indirecte.

Wenn man eine Küche ganz in Schwarz plant, muss man die grösstmögliche Anzahl Lichtquellen nutzten, natürliche oder künstliche, direkte oder indirekte.

TIPS - ASTUCES - TIPPS

- *Completely black kitchen furniture with a matt finish provides surprising and unconventional results.*
- *El mobiliario de cocina totalmente negro con acabado mate da un resultado sorprendente.*
- *Le mobilier d'une cuisine totalement noir avec des finitions mates donne des résultats surprenants et originaux.*
- *Eine vollständig schwarze Kücheneinrichtung mit einer matter Oberfläche hat eine erstaunliche Wirkung und ist unkonventionell.*

BEDROOMS

DORMITORIOS

CHAMBRES

SCHLAFZIMMER

Color performs a central role in defining a bedroom's style and providing an ambience to suit the tastes of its inhabitants. After all, it is the most personal place in the home. Some people prefer a tranquil atmosphere conducive to rest, while others are more inclined towards a livelier ambience characterized by energy and vitality.

Colors can be used to create micro-ambiences and give rise to a highly varied set of sensations in a given room. The tones of the bed, headboards and bedside tables may not be the same as the tones in the area for getting ready to go out or the area for reading, watching TV or eating. There is, of course, also the possibility of not dividing the space up into zones and giving the different spaces the same look to emphasize continuity by using a single tone.

The tones of the upholstery, curtains, bed linen and walls all make an important contribution in the décor, which is why the interplay between color and texture is so critical.

El color es fundamental para brindarle un estilo a la recámara y un ambiente que responda a las preferencias de sus habitantes, pues es el sitio más personal de la casa.

Hay quienes optan por la tranquilidad y por una atmósfera propicia para el reposo, mientras que otras personas prefieren que se perciba dinamismo y que el área se sienta con energía y vitalidad.

A través de los colores se pueden generar micro - ambientes y provocar las más diversas sensaciones en una habitación. La franja de descanso conformada por cama, cabeceras y burós podría tener tonalidades distintas a las del espacio destinado al arreglo o al que comúnmente se use para la lectura, para ver la TV o para consumir alimentos. Desde luego, también está la alternativa de no zonificar y que los espacios tengan un mismo aspecto reforzando la idea de continuidad a través de un solo matiz.

Son relevantes en el conjunto decorativo los tonos de las tapicerías y cortinajes, los de la ropa de cama y los muros; es por ello que juega también un papel significativo la interacción entre color y textura.

La couleur est fondamentale pour doter la chambre d'un certain style et d'une atmosphère particulière qui répondent aux attentes des occupants. La chambre est évidemment la pièce la plus personnelle de la maison.

Certains mettent en exergue sa tranquillité et essayent donc d'y établir une atmosphère propice au repos. D'autres préfèrent que l'on perçoive le dynamisme dans une pièce pleine d'énergie et de vitalité.

C'est par le biais des couleurs que l'on peut créer des micro-atmosphères et susciter des sensations variées dans une chambre. Le lieu de repos, composé du lit, du chevet et des tables de nuit, peut par exemple être de teintes différentes par rapport à celles de la pièce en général ou à celles destinées à l'espace - détente (pour lire, regarder la télé ou se restaurer). Bien sûr, on peut renoncer à aménager diverses zones et préférer un espace homogène dont on soulignera la continuité avec une seule couleur.

Mais n'oublions pas le rôle joué par les teintes des tissus de la literie, des rideaux, des tentures au mur, des tapis ou de la moquette et par leur texture qui interagit avec la couleur.

Die Farbe ist ein wesentlicher Faktor, um dem Schlafzimmer Stil zu verleihen und ein Ambiente, das den Vorlieben seiner Bewohner entspricht, da es der persönlichste Raum des Hauses ist.

Es gibt Personen, die sich für Ruhe und für eine Atmosphäre entscheiden, die zum Ausruhen geeignet ist, während andere es vorziehen, Dynamik zu spüren und dass der Bereich voll von Energie und Leben ist.

Durch die Farben kann man Mikro-Ambientes entstehen lassen und die verschiedendsten Empfindungen in einem Raum provozieren. Die Ruhezone, bestehend aus Bett, dessen Kopfteilen und Nachttischen, kann andere Farbtöne aufweisen als die Bereiche, die zum Zurechtmachen gedacht sind, oder die normalerweise zum Lesen, zum Fernsehen oder Essen bestimmt sind. Selbstverständlich besteht auch die Möglichkeit, nicht zu Unterteilen und alle Bereiche gleich zu halten, die Idee der Kontinuität durch nur einen einzigen Farbton verstärkend.

Im dekorativen Ensemble sind die Farbtöne der Bezüge und Vorhänge, der Bettwäsche und der Wände relevant; deshalb spielt auch die Wechselwirkung zwischen Farbe und Textur eine wichtige Rolle.

TIPS - ASTUCES - TIPPS

• *A refined setting can be created by combining two tones of white, one pigmented and the other pure.*
• *Al combinar dos tonos de blanco, uno pigmentado y otro puro, se consigue un contexto refinado.*
• *En associant deux blancs, l'un cassé et l'autre pur, on donne à la chambre un air très raffiné.*
• *Mit der Kombination von zwei Weisstönen, einer leicht gefärbt und der andere rein, erreicht man eine vornehme Umgebung.*

White monochrome settings enjoy an uninterrupted flow and their spaciousness is all the more pronounced.

Las atmósferas monocromáticas blanquecinas hacen que el espacio se perciba sin interrupciones y que luzca su dimensión.

Les atmosphères monochromes à base de blanc mettent en valeur la continuité de la pièce et ses dimensions.

Einfarbig weisse Einrichtungen lassen einen Raum ununterbrochen wirken und betonen seine Grösse.

TIPS - ASTUCES - TIPPS
• If pure white is the dominant color, an appealing contrast can be achieved with white accessories.
• Si se usa como dominante un blanco puro, el contraste con accesorios negros es muy atractivo.
• Si on choisit le blanc pur comme couleur dominante, le contraste avec le noir de certains accessoires n'en sera que plus séduisant.
• Wenn man hauptsächlich ein reines Weiss verwendet, ist der Kontrast zu schwarzen Dekorationsstücken sehr attraktiv.

Black and white decoration guarantees good results and helps emphasize certain planes.

Una decoración blanco y negro garantiza buenos resultados y ayuda a subrayar algunos planos.

Un design blanc et noir est la garantie d'une décoration réussie qui met en valeur certaines surfaces.

Eine schwarz weisse Dekoration garantiert ein gutes Ergebnis und hilft einige Grundrisse zu betonen.

TIPS - ASTUCES - TIPPS

• *Matt black leather headboards with a cushioned finish add elegance to the ambience.*

• *Las cabeceras de piel negra mate con acabados mullidos realzan la impresión de elegancia.*

• *Les têtes de lit en cuir noir, mates et moelleuses au toucher, renforcent la sensation d'élégance que l'on éprouve dans la chambre.*

• *Kopfstücke aus schwarzem matten Leder mit weicher Oberfläche unterstreichen den Eindruck von Eleganz.*

If the color white is prevalent on large surfaces and sizeable mirrors are added, there is greater luminosity and the area looks more spacious.

Cuando el color blanco sobresale en las grandes superficies y se añaden espejos de buen tamaño, aumenta la luminosidad y el área se percibe más amplia.

Lorsque le blanc est mis en valeur par de grandes surfaces que des miroirs complètent, la luminosité augmente et la pièce paraît plus grande.

Wenn Weiss auf den grossen Oberflächen vorherrscht und man grosse Spiegel hinzufügt, wird die Helligkeit erhöht und der Raum als grösser empfunden.

TIPS - ASTUCES - TIPPS
• *Blacks and browns look superb on cloth and leather with soft, silky textures.*
• *Los negros y cafés se ven soberbios en telas y pieles de texturas suaves y sedosas.*
• *Le noir et le marron sont magnifiques sur du cuir ou des tissus soyeux et doux au toucher.*
• *Schwarz- und Brauntöne wirken kostbar auf Stoffen und Leder mit weicher und seidiger Textur.*

A decorative scheme with two dark tones, such as black and brown, works wonderfully but requires generous inflows of light.

Une décoration basée sur deux couleurs foncées, comme le noir et le marron, est fabuleuse mais les sources de lumières doivent être assez importantes.

El decorado con dos tonos oscuros, como el café y el negro, es fabuloso, pero es necesario que las entradas de luz sean generosas.

Dekoration mit dunklen Farben, wie Braun und Schwarz, ist fabelhaft, aber es sollte reichlich Licht einfallen.

TIPS · ASTUCES · TIPPS

• *Combinations of more than four colors are now seen as a bold move that provides personality.*

• *Arriesgarse a combinar más de cuatro colores, es hoy un recurso que aporta personalidad.*

• *On n'hésite pas, de nos jours, à associer plus de 4 couleurs pour personnaliser une chambre.*

• *Zu riskieren mehr als vier Farben zu kombinieren, ist heutzutage ein Mittel einem Raum mehr Persönlichkeit zu geben.*

A wall headboard in this tone combines with the bed cover to lend the area its very own personality.

Un muro cabecera en rojo, en combinación con el cubre cama, le da personalidad al área.

Une cloison qui fait office de tête de lit, dont la couleur va avec celle du couvre lit, dote la chambre d'une petite touche personnelle.

Ein Wand als Kopfstück in diesem Farbton, kombiniert mit dem Bettüberwurf, gibt dem Bereich Persönlichkeit.

A wall covered by wallpaper sporting orange flowers adds vitality and distinction to the bedroom.
The mix of color, texture and patterns is highly decorative.

Un muro con tapizado de flores en color naranja realza la recámara y le da vitalidad. La mezcla de color, textura y dibujo es altamente decorativa.

Un mur tapissé par un motif floral orange met en valeur la chambre et lui donne de la vitalité. L'association entre couleur, texture et motif est très esthétique.

Eine Wand mit einer Tapete orangefarbener Blumen, verschönert das Schlafzimmer und gibt ihm Lebendigkeit. Die Mischung aus Farbe, Textur und Zeichnung ist hochdekorativ.

TIPS - ASTUCES - TIPPS

- Orange and brown together produce a tried and tested contrast and a sensation of warmth.
- El naranja y el café es uno de los contrastes más probados, que activa la sensación de calidez.
- L'orange et le marron garantissent un des contrastes les plus réussis qui existent et réchauffent une chambre.
- Orange und Braun ist eine der meisterprobtesten Kontraste, der ein Gefühl von Wärme auslöst.

TIPS - ASTUCES - TIPPS
- The color code in kids' rooms tends to favor bright and saturated colors.
- El código cromático en las habitaciones infantiles es hacia los colores luminosos y saturados.
- Les conventions en matière de couleurs pour les chambres d'enfants vont vers des teintes lumineuses et saturées.
- Der Farbcode in Kinderzimmern geht in Richtung leuchtender, konzentrierter Farben.

A notable visual effect is achieved by blending dark wood furniture, brown and white bed covers and pillow cases and fuchsia curtains.

Le design du mobilier en bois foncé, la literie blanche et marron foncé et les rideaux fuchsia constituent une réussite visuelle impressionnante.

El diseño del mobiliario en madera oscura, la ropa de cama en chocolate y blanco, y el cortinaje fucsia posee un gran impacto visual.

Das Design der Möbel in dunklem Halz, die Bettwäsche in Braun und Weiss und die Vorhänge in Fuchsie, haben eine starke optische Wirkung.

TIPS · ASTUCES · TIPPS
• A pure white translucent inner curtain underscores and illuminates the fuchsia of the outer curtain.
• Una cortina interior translúcida en blanco puro hace que sobresalga y se ilumine el fucsia de la cortina exterior.
• Un rideau intérieur blanc pur et translucide illumine et fait ressortir l'esthétique de celui, extérieur, de couleur fuchsia.
• Eine durchsichtige Gardine in reinem Weiss lässt den Vorhang in Fuchsie herausstechen und wie beleuchtet erscheinen.

Violet tones such as indigo, lilac and purple are very comfortable in the bedroom because they are created in a balanced blend of red and blue.

Los matices del violeta como el índigo, lila y morado son muy confortables en la recámara, pues provienen de la mezcla equilibrada del rojo y el azul.

Produits équilibrés du bleu et du rouge, les teintes dérivées du violet, comme l'indigo, le lilas et le mauve sont recommandées dans une chambre.

Die Schattierungen des Violett wie Indigo, Lila und Dunkelviolett sind sehr angenehm im Schlafzimmer, da sie aus der ausgewogenen Mischung von Blau und Rot entstehen.

TIPS - ASTUCES - TIPPS

• A lilac rug placed in a neutral atmosphere makes for a harmonious and peaceful setting.

• Con la introducción de un tapete lila en una atmósfera neutra se consigue un escenario armónico y en calma.

• Avec un tapis de couleur lilas dans une atmosphère neutre, le décor devient harmonieux et paisible.

• Mit dem Einbringen eines lila Teppichs in eine neutrale Atmosphäre erreicht man eine harmonische, ruhige Szenerie.

BATHROOMS
BAÑOS
SALLES DE BAIN
BADEZIMMER

When it comes to decorating the bathroom, white is one of the most highly valued tones among architects and interior designers thanks to its great qualities including the sensation of cleanliness, order and hygiene it offers. Furniture makers also make a lot of bathtubs, toilets, bidets and washbasins in this color.

Natural stone is also a major presence in the bathroom, in particular on surfaces, walls and floors. Its tones and veining therefore need to be taken into consideration. The same goes for wood, with which cabinets housing washbasins are made.

A color pallet based on aluminum, steel and other chromed materials makes its mark on the décor, as do other things like mirror surfaces, the tone of the light and of anything else in the area including the towels.

Bathrooms used on a daily basis tend to be more conservative than bathrooms for visitors, which is where more daring color options are used with current trends opting for strong tones and contrasts.

Debido a sus grandes cualidades, la sensación de limpieza, nitidez e higiene que ofrece, el blanco es sin duda uno de los matices preferidos por los arquitectos e interioristas para la decoración de baños. Los productores de muebles también fabrican una buena proporción de tinas, inodoros, bidés y lavabos en este color.

Del mismo modo, las piedras naturales son materiales constantes en estos espacios, muy usadas en cubiertas, muros y pisos, por lo que hay que considerar sus tonos y los de sus veteados, al igual que los de la madera, con la que se suelen hacer los bajo lavabos.

Cuentan también en el diseño de la paleta cromática la tonalidad del aluminio, el acero y demás materiales cromados, así como las superficies de espejos, el tono de la luz, y de cualquier otro elemento que se encuentre en el área, incluyendo las toallas.

Por lo general, los baños de uso cotidiano son más conservadores que los de visitas, en estos últimos se suele experimentar con soluciones más atrevidas en cuanto a color se refiere, y la tendencia es hacia los contrastes y los tonos fuertes.

En vertu de ses qualités intrinsèques, de cette sensation de propreté, d'ordre et de salubrité qu'il dégage, le blanc est sans nul doute une des couleurs de prédilection des architectes et des décorateurs d'intérieurs pour habiller une salle de bain. En outre, les fabricants de meubles produisent un nombre élevé de baignoires, W.C., bidets et autres lavabos dans cette couleur.

La pierre naturelle est également un des matériaux communs à ces pièces que l'on utilise très fréquemment pour les revêtements, les murs et le sol. Il faut donc prendre en compte ses reflets et ses veines naturelles, tout comme celles du bois que l'on emploie pour fabriquer des meubles sous lavabo.

L'aluminium, l'acier et autres matériaux chromés, jouent, quant à eux, un rôle dans la palette chromatique tout comme la surface des miroirs, le reflet de la lumière et d'autres éléments présents dans la pièce comme, par exemple, les serviettes.

La décoration des salles de bain que l'on utilise tous les jours est, en général, classique alors que celle des salles de bain réservées aux visites est plus audacieuse de par ses couleurs et on cherchera davantage à créer des contrastes et à utiliser des teintes vives.

Aufgrund seiner Eigenschaften, den Eindruck von Sauberkeit, Reinheit und Hygiene, den es bietet, ist Weiss ohne Zweifel eine der bevorzugten Farbtöne der Architekten und Innendekorateure für die Dekoration eines Badezimmers. Es werden auch eine grosse Auswahl an Badewannen, Toiletten, Bidets und Waschbecken in dieser Farbe produziert.

Genauso sind Natursteine Materialien, die konstant in Badezimmern verwendet werden, sie werden oft für Abdeckungen, Wände und Böden benutzt, weshalb man die Schattierungen und Maserungen beachten sollte, genauso wie die des Holzes, das üblicherweise für die Unterschränke der Waschbecken benutzt wird.

Bei der Planung des Farbspektrums zählen auch die Farben des Aluminiums, Stahls und anderer verchromter Materialen, die Oberflächen der Spiegel, der Farbton des Lichts und jedes andere Element, das sich im Bereich befindet, einschliesslich der Handtücher.

Normalerweise sind die Badezimmer, die täglich benutzt werden, konservativer als die Gästebadezimmer; in den letzteren neigt man eher zu Experimenten mit gewagteren Lösungen in den Farben und die Tendenz geht dort zu Kontrasten und kräftigen Farben.

TIPS - ASTUCES - TIPPS

- • A monochrome bathroom limited to different intensities of white is an impeccable space.
- • Un baño monocromático, limitado a blanco en varias intensidades, genera un espacio inmaculado.
- • Une salle de bain monochrome, limitée à des dégradés de blanc, donne à la pièce un air immaculé.
- • Ein einfarbiges Badezimmer, auf Weiss in verschiedener Intensität beschränkt, schafft einen makellosen Raum.

TIPS - ASTUCES - TIPPS

• Bathrooms in dark tones are not very common, but they are stylish and modern in appearance.

• Los baños en tonos oscuros son una opción poco común y su apariencia es moderna y elegante.

• Les salles de bain foncées sont peu communes mais leur apparence est à la fois moderne et élégante.

• Badezimmer in dunklen Farben sind eine ungewöhnliche Option und sehen modern und elegant aus.

TIPS - ASTUCES - TIPPS

- As neutral as it may be, contact with light brings out the coloring and expressiveness of materials.
- Por neutro que sea, el colorido y la expresividad de los materiales se realza al contacto con la luz.
- Bien que le coloris soit neutre, les teintes employées et les matériaux ressortent bien au contact de la lumière.
- So neutral sie auch sein mögen, die Farben und die Ausdruckskraft der Materialien werden durch den Kontakt mit Licht verschönert

Stone walls in cream tones brighten up the mirror area and provide a frame for a prominent black surface on a wooden item of furniture.

Los muros pétreos en matices cremas le dan luminosidad al área del espejo y sirven de marco a una protagónica cubierta negra que está sobre un mueble de madera.

Les couleurs crème des murs en pierre naturelle éclairent la zone du miroir et encadrent l'élément principal de la pièce, le revêtement noir qui couronne un meuble en bois.

Wände aus Stein in Cremetönen geben dem Bereich um den Spiegel herum Helligkeit und umrahmen eine auffällige schwarze Platte, die auf einem Holzmöbel ruht.

Wood creates a splendid contrast with white ceramic washbasins and a white marble surface, while stone tones blend well with the color beige.

La madera contrasta bien con lavabos cerámicos blancos y una cubierta de mármol blanco, mientras que el color pétreo armoniza con el color beige.

Le bois contraste bien avec les lavabos en céramique blanche et le revêtement en marbre de la même couleur tandis que celle de la pierre s'harmonise avec le beige.

Das Holz bildet einen guten Kontrast zu den weissen Waschbecken und einer Platte aus weissem Marmor, während die Steinfarbe mit der Farbe Beige harmoniert.

TIPS · ASTUCES · TIPPS
- *Soft yellow light provides the bathroom with a serene and cozy feel.*
- *La luz amarilla y suave coopera a darle serenidad a un lugar y hace que se sienta acogedor.*
- *La lumière jaune et douce participe à l'impression de sérénité et de confort qui se dégage de la pièce.*
- *Gelbes, weiches Licht trägt dazu bei einem Ort Ruhe zu verleihen und lässt ihn einladend wirken.*

The difference in tones between a slab and natural stone provides a solid basis for creating attractive color schemes.

La inexactitud tonal entre una loseta y otra de piedra natural, representa una oportunidad para crear atractivos esquemas cromáticos.

Les légères différences de couleur entre les dalles et la pierre naturelle sont une bonne occasion pour mettre au point de séduisants motifs chromatiques.

Die Ungleichheit der Farbtöne der einzelnen Natursteinplatten, bietet die Möglichkeit attraktive Farbmuster zu schaffen.

The wall housing the washbasin becomes all the more eye-catching and vibrant if it is painted or coated in a bright color.

La pared en donde se ubica el lavabo es la que más llama la atención, si se pinta o reviste en un color vivo la percepción de dinamismo se eleva.

Le mur supportant le lavabo est celui est que l'on regarde d'abord. Si on le peint ou si on le tapisse avec une couleur vive, la sensation de dynamisme s'accroît encore.

Die Wand, an der sich das Waschbecken befindet, ist die auffälligste; wenn man sie in einer lebendigen Farbe streicht oder verkleidet, wird der Eindruck von Dynamik verstärkt.

TIPS - ASTUCES - TIPPS
• A contemporary bathroom in red and black is appealing and even sensual.
• Un baño contemporáneo en rojo y negro es llamativo y puede resultar sensual.
• Une salle de bain moderne rouge et noire est voyante mais elle peut également être très sensuelle.
• Ein zeitgenössisches Badezimmer in Rot und Schwarz erregt Aufmerksamkeit und kann sinnlich wirken.

Rosewood wallpaper is a good choice in the bathroom, especially when used in combination with the mirror and the washbasin with its respective item of furniture in brown and black.

Se pueden tapizar los muros en palo de rosa y colocar en torno a ellos el espejo, el lavabo y su correspondiente mueble en café y negro.

Il est possible de tapisser les murs en rose pale et y placer un miroir, le lavabo et son meuble marron et noir qui va avec.

Man kann die Wände mit einer rosa Tapete mit schwarzem Blumenmuster verkleiden und mehrere Spiegel anbringen, das Waschbecken und sein Unterschrank sind schwarz und braun.

TIPS - ASTUCES - TIPPS
- A soft color on all the walls together with large mirrors creates the impression that the color is invading the area.
- Con un color suave en todos los muros y grandes espejos se obtiene la sensación de que el color invade el área.
- Avec une teinte suave sur tous les murs et de grands miroirs, on a comme l'impression que la couleur envahit littéralement l'espace.
- Mit einer sanften Farbe an den Wänden und grossen Spiegeln erreicht man, dass die Farbe den Bereich zu überströmen scheint.

The combined tones of mahogany and gray woods on the furniture and floor contrast superbly with the electric blue on the walls.

La combinación tonal de las maderas caoba y agrisada en mobiliario y piso contrastan estupendo con el azul eléctrico en muros.

L'association chromatique de bois acajou et gris pale pour le mobilier et le sol contraste magnifiquement avec le bleu électrique sur les murs.

Die Farbkombination der Hölzer in Kaoba und einem Grauton bei den Möbeln und dem Boden stehen in einem herrlichen Kontrast zu dem elektrisierenden Blau der Wände.

TIPS - ASTUCES - TIPPS
• *Blue is a cold color, which makes it ideal for a bathroom flooded with sunlight.*
• *El azul es un color frío, lo que le convierte en muy adecuado para un baño dotado con luz natural.*
• *Étant donné que le bleu est une couleur froide, il convient très bien dans une salle de bain éclairée par de la lumière naturelle.*
• *Blau ist eine kalte Farbe, was es sehr gut in ein Badezimmer mit viel natürlichem Licht passen lässt.*

The warmth
of red wood
balances the
coldness of
furniture topped
with marble.

La calidez de
una madera
rojiza nivela la
apreciación de
frialdad que
puede dar un
mueble con
cubierta de
mármol.

La sensation de
chaleur dégagée
par un bois rouge-
brun atténue celle
de froid que peut
produire un meuble
recouvert de marbre.

Die Wärme des
rötlichen Holzes
gleicht die Kälte
aus, die ein
Möbelstück mit
einer Marmorplatte
ausstrahlen kann.

TIPS - ASTUCES - TIPPS

- One decorative option is to use colored glass or panes with a film of color.
- Una opción decorativa consiste en entintar un vidrio o colocarle una película de color.
- Teinter du verre et ou le recouvrir d'une fine pellicule colorée est une solution décorative qui a son charme.
- Eine Glasfläche zu färben oder eine farbige Folie auf ihr anzubringen ist eine Option in der Dekoration.

architecture   arquitectónicos   architectoniques   architektonische

photography   fotográficos   photographiques   fotografische

Editado en Julio del 2010. Impreso en China.
El cuidado de edición estuvo a cargo de
AM Editores S.A. de C.V. Edited in July 2010.
Printed in China. Published by AM Editores
S.A. de C.V.